Why Just

have passed sir

published more and more people have requested a book of Just Casseroles. And so this book was launched.

Casseroles are ideal for today's life style: many, if not all, can be adapted to modern kitchen appliances; they suit anyone's income and many can be frozen or prepared ahead to fit busy schedules. Generally, casseroles are highly recommended for their dietary completeness and for the flexibility they provide.

Here then, is a wide assortment of appetizing dishes, all tested and waiting for your approval. Present a casserole to your family and friends and round out your menu with a fresh salad and a muffin . . . great eating!

Thankyou to all who have made Just Muffins the success that it has been. I hope Just Casseroles will meet your expectations.

Sincerely,

Gaye Hansen

B.H.Ec.

North Vancouver, 1981

Books in the 'Just Series'
over 100,000 in print

Just Muffins 1978

Just Casseroles 1981

Just for Tea 1982

Just Cookies 1984

Just Muffins
674 St. Ives Cr.
North Vancouver, B.C.
V7N 2X3

Printed by Cranbrook Litho Press Ltd.
Cranbrook, B.C.

ISBN 0-9691644-1-6

Printed in Canada

Table of Contents

Eggs and Cheese

Fish and Seafood

Poultry

Meats

Baked Eggs Forestière

M.	Imp.	
4	4	slices back bacon
125 ml	½ c	chopped onion
450 g	1-lb	fresh mushrooms, sliced
15 ml	1 T	flour
125 ml	½ c	chicken broth
125 ml	½ c	light cream
6	6	eggs

Cut bacon in strips and fry with onions and mushrooms. Stir in flour broth and cream. Turn into a pie plate. Make hollows for the eggs and break the eggs into the nests. Bake until eggs are set.

Bake: 180° (350°)
Time: 15-20 min.
Serves: 6

Egg and Green Bean Bake

M.	Imp.	
450 g	1-lb	fresh green beans or equivalent, cooked, drained
30 ml	2T	butter
45 ml	3T	whole wheat flour or all purpose flour
125 ml	1/2c	milk
7ml	1 1/2t	honey
1 ml	1/4t	salt
350 ml	1 1/2c	yogurt
4	4	hard cooked eggs, chopped
450 ml	2c	grated swiss cheese
60 ml	1/4c	bread crumbs
15 ml	1T	melted butter

Make a sauce of the 30 ml (2T) butter, flour, milk. Stir in honey, salt and yogurt and remove from heat. Layer beans, eggs and cheese in a casserole and pour sauce over all. Top with combined bread crumbs and melted butter.

Bake: 180° (350°)
Time: 20 min
Serves: 4-6

Baked Eggs Cebolla

Cebolla is a Spanish word for onion

M.	Imp.	
4	4	slices bacon, cut into 2 cm (1") pieces
1	1	onion, chopped
5 ml	1 t	snipped parsley
4	4	eggs
		salt and pepper to taste
125 ml	1/2 c	grated swiss cheese
4-8	4-8	slices buttered toast

Fry bacon and onion until thoroughly cooked. Drain off excess fat. Sprinkle parsley over; break eggs over top; season and sprinkle cheese over. Cover and cook slowly until eggs are set. Place on toast to serve with toast triangles along side.

Serves: 4

Baked Omelet

M.	Imp.	
4	4	slices bacon, halved
30 ml	2T	chopped onion
10 ml	2t	snipped parsley
4	4	eggs
1 ml	1/4t	celery salt
1 ml	1/4t	salt
		pepper to taste
125 ml	1/2c	light cream
225 ml	1 c	grated Swiss cheese
		paprika

Fry bacon until cooked but not crisp. Sauté onions in drippings. Spread onions and parsley in a pie plate. Beat eggs, seasonings and cream; pour over onions. Top with bacon slices and shredded cheese. Sprinkle with paprika. Bake until eggs are set and cheese is melted.

Bake: 180° (350°)
Time: 15 min
Serves: 4

Eggs in Ramekins

For each serving you will need:

M.	Imp.	
30 ml	2T	bread crumbs
10 ml	2t	margarine
1	1	slice tomato cut 1cm (1/2")
1	1	egg
30 ml	2T	grated swiss cheese
15 ml	1T	cream

Lightly fry bread crumbs in the margarine, just to crisp. Place in the bottom of a ramekin; top with tomato slice then egg. Season with salt and pepper. Top with cheese and cream. Bake until eggs are set

Variation

• Eggs baked in tomatoes • scoop out pulp from a tomato. Break egg into tomato and top with cheese and buttered bread crumbs

Bake: 180° (350°)
Time: 15-20 min
Serves: 1

Baked Eggs over Corned Beef Hash

An excellent item for the brunch menu

M.	Imp.	
340 ml	1 - 12 oz	can corned beef
4	4	potatoes, cooked, cut up
60 ml	1/4 c	margarine
60 ml	1/4 c	green oinons, chopped
6	6	eggs
90 ml	6T	light cream

Fry cut up potatoes in hot butter, turning occasionally. Add green onions and continue to fry until potatoes are lightly browned. Add chopped up corned beef and continue to cook until heated (do not cover) Place corned beef miytore into a shallow casserole. Make 6 hollows in the hash, dot with butter and slip one egg into each hollow. Top each egg with 15 ml (1T) cream.

Bake: 180° (350°)
Time: 15 - 20
Serves: 6

Tomato-Cheese Pie

Good at brunch, lunch and supper; hot or cold; at home or at the picnic grounds

M.	Imp.	
1	1	pastry shell, baked
450 g	1-lb	Gruyère cheese, thinly sliced
2-3	2-3	large tomatoes cut in 1cm (½") slices
		salt and pepper
5 ml	1 t	basil
30 ml	2 T	grated Parmesan cheese
30 ml	2 T	melted butter

Sprinkle tomato slices with salt and let them drain for 30 min. Arrange cheese slices in pie shell and the tomato slices on top. Sprinkle with pepper, basil, Parmesan cheese and melted butter. Bake until lightly browned.

Bake: 190° (375°)
Time: 25 min
Serves: 6

Noodles Romanoff

M.	Imp.	
125 g	4 oz	wide noodles, cooked
30 ml	2T	finely chopped onion
30 ml	2T	butter or margarine
225 g	1 c	cottage cheese
225 g	1 c	sour cream
f.g.	f.g.	garlic powder
1 ml	1/4 t	celery salt
2 ml	1/2 t	salt
5 ml	1 t	worcestershire sauce
60 ml	1/4 c	bread crumbs
60 ml	1/4 c	grated Parmesan cheese

Sauté onion in butter until tender. Combine with noodles, cottage cheese, sour cream, garlic, celery salt, salt and worcestershire sauce. Turn into a greased casserole. Top with bread crumbs and cheese.

Variation

• Stroganoff Casserole • brown 450 g (1-lb) ground beef with onions. Drain off excess fat if necessary and continue as above.

Bake: 180°(350°)
Time: 30 min
Serves: 6

Cheese Strata

M.	Imp.	
8	8	slices bread
4	4	slices process cheese
5 ml	1t	salt
2	2	eggs
450 ml	2 c	hot milk
dash	dash	paprika

Arrange 4 slices of bread in a square baking pan. Place over each slice of bread one slice of cheese and then another bread slice. Combine remaining ingredients and pour over; bake until set.

Variations

- Sausage Strata • add 450 g (1-lb) browned sausage meat to the cheese layer
- Tuna Strata • add one 200 g (7 oz) can tuna, sautéed onion and a pinch of oregano. Try mozzarella cheese slices.
- stratas may also include cooked diced chicken, turkey, fish, seafood and cooked vegetables.

Bake: 190° (375°)
Time: 45 min
Serves: 4

Cheese Strata Special

An elegant version

M.	Imp.	
75 ml	1/3 c	margarine
1	1	minced garlic clove
2 ml	1/2 t	dry mustard
8-10	8-10	slices bread
450 ml	2 c	shredded sharp cheddar
15 ml	1 T	parsley flakes
5 ml	1 t	salt
2 ml	1/2 t	worcestershire sauce
4	4	eggs
550 ml	2 1/3 c	milk
150 ml	2/3 c	dry white wine

Blend margarine, garlic, mustard; spread on one side of each slice of bread. Place bread, buttered side down in a square baking dish. Toss together the cheese, parsley, salt and worcestershire and spread evenly over bread. Place remaining bread slices over top. Beat eggs add milk and wine; pour over bread. Cover and refrigerate 2 hr or overnight. Bake until set.

Bake 160° (325°)
Time: 1 1/4 hr
Serves: 4

Quiche

A delicious savory flan with a multitude of variations

M.	Imp	
1	1	unbaked pie shell
8	8	slices bacon, diced and cooked crisp
350 ml	1½ c	grated swiss cheese
3	3	eggs
225 ml	1 c	cream
125 ml	½ c	milk
2 ml	½ t	salt
1 ml	¼ t	pepper
f.g.	f.g.	cayenne
2 ml	½ t	dry mustard

Line the pie shell with the cheese and bacon. Combine remaining ingredients and beat well. Pour over cheese and bacon. Bake until firm.

Bake: 190° (375°)
Time: 45 min
Serves: 6

Quiche Variations

Follow the same general instructions as for Quiche

Fish Quiche

225 ml	1 c	grated swiss cheese
200 g	1 - 7 oz	can fish such as tuna, shrimp, salmon, crab etc.
85 g	1 - 3½ oz	can French onion rings (use half in the filling, half for a topping)
225 ml	1 c	grated swiss cheese
3	3	eggs
225 ml	1 c	sour cream
2 ml	½ t	worcestershire sauce
1 ml	¼ t	salt
f.g.	f.g.	pepper

Cottage Cheese Quiche

450 ml	2 c	cottage cheese
125 ml	½ c	grated swiss cheese
2	2	eggs
15 - 30 ml	1 - 2 T	snipped chives, green onions or parsley
125 ml	½ c	French onion rings (topping)

Quiche Variations (cont'd)

Spinach Quiche

125 ml	1/2 c	grated swiss cheese
350 ml	1 1/2 c	cottage cheese
75 ml	1/3 c	light cream
4	4	eggs
7 ml	1 1/2 t	salt
f.g.	f.g.	pepper
dash	dash	nutmeg
340 g	1 - 12 oz	package spinach, cooked, drained and chopped
30 ml	2 T	snipped chives

Bake the pie shell 3 min. in a 240° (475°) oven; fill pie shell and bake until firm.

More Variations

Any number or combination of ingredients can be used in a quiche:

mushrooms • lightly sautéed
cheese variations • feta, cheddar
asparagus • precook
leek, broccoli, cauliflower • cooked
ham • diced
olives • sliced
sausage • browned
onion • sautéed
any seafood or fish
seasonings • add an herb or spice

Cheese Soufflé

M.	Imp.	
90 ml	6T	butter or margarine
75 ml	1/3c	flour
2 ml	1/2t	salt
350 ml	1 1/2c	milk
700 ml	3c	grated cheese such as Swiss, cheddar
6	6	egg yolks
6	6	egg whites

Melt butter, blend in flour and salt. Add milk and stir until thickened. Remove from heat and stir in cheese. Stir until cheese is melted. Beat egg yolks until thick and stir into cheese sauce. Cool slightly. Fold in stiffly beaten egg whites. Turn into a soufflé dish. Run a knife around the dish 3 cm (1") from edge to a 3cm (1") depth for a high hat soufflé.

Bake: 190° (375°)
Time: 30 min.
Serves: 6

Soufflé Variations

Finnish Meat Soufflé

- stir 250 - 450 ml (1-2c) browned ground beef into the cheese mixture

Seafood Soufflé

- add 250 ml (1c) flaked tuna, salmon, shrimp, lobster or cooked fish to the cheese mixture

Other suggestions

- add 250 ml (1c) of any cooked vegetable such as
  - broccoli
  - mushrooms
  - spinach
  - corn
- add 250 ml (1c) cooked
  - ham
  - chicken
  - turkey

Seven Minute Tuna

M.	Imp.	
85 g	1 - 3½ oz	can French fried onions
200 g	1 - 7 oz	can tuna
175 ml	3/4 c	thinly sliced celery
60 ml	¼ c	green pepper
1 ml	¼ t	onion powder
125 ml	½ c	sliced mushrooms
284 ml	1 - 10 oz	can cream of celery soup

Combine half the onions with the remaining ingredients and place in a greased casserole. Bake 25 min. Sprinkle remaining onions over top and bake 5 min. longer.

Bake: 180° (350°)
Time: 30 min.
Serves: 4

Quick Cheesy Tuna Bake

M.	Imp.	
200 g	1-7oz	can tuna
450 ml	2 c	cooked rice
30 ml	2T	margarine
30 ml	2T	flour
2 ml	1/2t	salt
225 ml	1 c	milk
284 ml	1-10 oz	cream of mushroom soup
60 ml	1/4c	mayonnaise
60 ml	1/4c	dry white wine
225 ml	1 c	cottage cheese
15 ml	1T	lemon juice
15 ml	1T	parsley flakes

Make a sauce of the margarine, flour, salt and milk; combine with tuna, rice and remaining ingredients. Bake until bubbly and heated through.

Bake: 180°(350°)
Time: 30 min.
Serves: 6

Tuna Rice Pie

Rice Shell

M.	Imp	
450 ml	2c	cooked rice
30 ml	2T	margarine
15 ml	1T	chopped onion
1 ml	1/4t	marjoram
15 ml	1T	parsley flakes
1	1	egg, slightly beaten

Sauté onion in the margarine until tender. Combine all the ingredients and line a pie plate as for pastry

Tuna Filling

200g	1 - 7oz	can tuna, drained
3	3	eggs, beaten
225 ml	1 c	milk
225 ml	1 c	shredded swiss cheese
1 ml	1/4t	salt
f.g.	f.g.	pepper
10 ml	2t	parsley
1 ml	1/4t	marjoram

Spread tuna evenly over rice shell. Combine remaining ingredients and pour over tuna.

Variations

- try cooked poultry, seafood, ham or other fish in place of tuna.

Bake: 180° (350°)
Time: 55 min
Serves: 6

Tuna Pot Pie

M.	Imp.	
175 ml	3/4c	diced celery
225 ml	1 c	chopped onion
45 ml	3T	margarine
2 ml	1/2t	tarragon
1 ml	1/4t	thyme
45 ml	3T	flour
225 ml	1 c	light cream
225 ml	1 c	fresh mushrooms, sliced
15 ml	1T	margarine
125 ml	1/2c	mayonnaise
15 ml	1T	lemon juice
15 ml	1T	dry white wine
2 ml	1/2t	salt
400g	2-7oz	cans tuna, drained
250 g	1-9oz	package frozen artichokes cooked, drained
350 ml	1 1/2 c	biscuit mix
75 ml	1/3c	water or milk

Cook celery and onion in the 45 ml (3T) margarine until tender. Add tarragon, thyme and flour. Add cream; cook until thickened. Add mushrooms sautéed in the 15 ml (1T) margarine. Stir in the mayonnaise, lemon, wine and salt. Fold in tuna and artichokes. Combine biscuit mix and water, knead 10 times; roll to 1 cm (1/2") thickness and cut into circles. Place on top. Bake: 190° (375°)

Time: 25 min

Serves: 6

Italian Tuna Casserole

M.	Imp.	
125 ml	1/2 c	chopped onion
30 ml	2T	margarine
284 ml	1 - 10 oz	can mushroom soup
150 ml	2/3 c	light cream or evaporated milk
75 ml	1/3 c	grated Parmesan cheese
200 g	1 - 7 oz	can tuna, drained and broken up
125 ml	1/2 c	sliced mushrooms
60 ml	1/4 c	sliced black olives
30 ml	2T	snipped parsley
10 ml	2t	lemon juice
450 ml	2c	noodles, cooked, drained

Sauté onion in margarine until tender. Add soup, cream, cheese and heat through. Add remaining ingrediants and pour into a deep casserole. Garnish with additional Parmesan and paprika if desired.

Bake: 180° (350°)
Time: 30 min.
Serves: 6

Aunty Jean's Crab Casserole

M.	Imp.	
200 g	1 - 7 oz	can crab
15 ml	1 T	lemon juice
284 ml	1 - 10 oz	can cream chicken soup
175 ml	3/4 c	mayonnaise
225 ml	1 c	chopped celery
15 ml	1 T	chopped green onion
125 ml	1/2 c	slivered almonds
2 ml	1/2 t	pepper
3	3	hard cooked eggs, chopped
225 ml	1 c	bread crumbs
30 ml	2 T	melted margarine

Drizzle lemon juice over the crab. Gently stir in the soup, mayonnaise, celery, green onion, almonds, pepper and eggs. Place in a greased casserole and top with bread crumbs combined with the melted margarine. Bake.

Variations

- substitute cooked chicken, turkey, tuna, salmon or other cooked seafood for the crab

Bake: 190° (375°)
Time: 30 min
Serves: 4

Seafood Exotica

M.	Imp.	
60 ml	2T	butter
350 ml	1½c	rice
125 ml	½c	slivered almonds, toasted
284 ml	1 - 10 oz	can chicken broth
		water
5 ml	1t	salt
60 ml	¼c	butter
350 ml	1½c	sliced mushrooms
10 ml	2t	curry
2 ml	½t	ginger
450 g	1 - lb	seafood such as crab, shrimp, lobster or a combination
60 ml	¼c	sherry
45 ml	3T	butter
60 ml	¼c	flour
2 ml	½t	salt
f.g.	f.g.	pepper
1 ml	¼t	dry mustard
700 ml	3c	light cream
225 ml	1c	grated swiss cheese

Seafood Exotica (cont'd)

Melt the 30 ml (2T) butter; add rice and stir until well coated. Add chicken broth plus sufficient water to make 700 ml (3 c) liquid. Stir in 5 ml (1t) salt and f.g. pepper and cook 20 min. Stir in the toasted almonds. Place in the bottom of a greased 23 X 33 cm (9 X 13") casserole.

Meanwhile sauté the mushrooms in the 60 ml (4T) butter. Add the curry and ginger; cook 3 min. Place over the cooked rice. Arrange seafood over the mushrooms and spoon over the sherry.

Make a cream sauce: melt the 45 ml (3T) butter. Stir in the flour, 2 ml (½t) salt, f.g. pepper and mustard. Gradually add the light cream; stir until thickened. Pour the sauce over the seafood. Top with grated cheese. Bake.

Bake: 205° (400°)
Time: 25 min
Serves: 10

Layered Fish Dinner

M.	Imp.	
45 ml	3T	margarine
175 ml	3/4c	chopped onions
450 ml	2c	grated raw potatoes
250 ml	1 c	grated raw carrots
225 ml	1c	cooked rice
225 ml	1c	chopped celery
450 g	1-1b	cut up fish fillets
450 ml	2 c	canned tomatoes
5 ml	1t	salt
1 ml	1/4t	pepper
100 ml	1/2c	bread crumbs
30 ml	2T	margarine, melted

Sauté the onions in the 45 ml (3T) margarine until clear. In a greased casserole arrange layers of potatoes, carrots, rice, celery, fish, tomatoes and onions seasoning each layer with salt and pepper. Top with the bread crumbs combined with the 30 ml (2T) margarine

Bake: 190° (375°)
Time: 1 hr
Serves: 6

Paella

M.	Imp.	
1½ kg	3-4 lb	chicken pieces
60 ml	¼ c	oil
125 ml	½ c	chopped onion
3	3	tomatoes, peeled, chopped
1	1	minced garlic clove
5 ml	1 t	paprika
15 ml	1 T	parsley flakes
5 ml	1 t	seasoned salt
.5 ml	⅛ t	saffron
2 ml	½ t	salt
350 ml	1½ c	rice
350 ml	3 c	water, hot
3	3	chicken bouillon cubes
250 g	1 - 9 oz	package frozen artichokes cooked and drained
1	1	pimiento sliced
350 ml	1½ c	frozen peas
340 g	¾ lb	cooked shrimp

Brown chicken pieces in hot oil; remove from the skillet. To remaining oil add onion, tomatoes and garlic; cook until tender. Stir in paprika, parsley, seasoned salt, saffron, salt, rice, water and bouillon cubes. Top with chicken and simmer 45 min. Add artichokes, pimiento, peas, shrimp. Cook 15 min.

Time: 1 hr
Serves: 6

Couillbac

An inviting hot fish pie of Russian origin; it's really very tasty.

M.	Imp.	
45 ml	3T.	butter
675 g	1½ lb.	red snapper or other fish fillets cut in pieces
225 ml	1 c	cooked rice
45 ml	3T	snipped parsley
60 ml	¼ c	finely chopped onion
		salt and pepper to taste
250 ml	1 c	sliced mushrooms
3	3	hard cooked eggs, chopped
90 ml	6T	melted butter
60-120 ml	¼ - ½ c	dry white wine
½	½	package frozen puff pastry
1	1	egg
5 ml	1t	oil
2 ml	½t	salt
f.g.	f.g.	pepper

Couillbac (cont'd)

Heat the 45 ml (3T) butter in a skillet and cook the fish pieces 3 min. Remove fish. In the same skillet, sauté the onion until transparent. Combine the rice and parsley and place half of it in a greased pie plate. Layer half of the fish and half the onion over the rice. Sprinkle with salt and pepper. Next put half of mushrooms and chopped egg. Repeat all the layers. Pour melted butter and wine over all.

Roll out puff pastry to fit pie plate and place on top of casserole. Trim. Combine the egg, oil, salt and pepper. Brush over top of pastry. Bake.

Bake: 205° (400°)
Time: 50 min.
Serves: 8

Baked Snapper Superb

M.	Imp.	
675 g	1½ lb	red snapper fillets
½	½	lemon, juiced
		salt
		pepper
		paprika
30 ml	2T	butter
350 ml	1½ c	fresh sliced mushrooms
45 ml	3T	butter
45 ml	3T	flour
300 ml	1¼ c	milk
60 ml	¼ c	dry white wine
2 ml	½ t	salt
3	3	hard cooked eggs, chopped
225 ml	1 c	cooked shrimp
225 ml	1 c	grated swiss cheese

Baked Snapper Superb (cont'd)

Cut fish into serving size pieces and place in a greased shallow casserole without overlapping. Sprinkle fish with lemon juice, salt, pepper and paprika. Bake at 205° (400°) 10 min. and remove from the oven.

Meanwhile sauté the mushrooms in the 30 ml (2T) butter. Make a white sauce of the 45 ml (3T) butter, flour, milk and 2 ml (½t) salt. Stir in wine. Fold in chopped eggs.

Drain off juices from the fish and stir into sauce. Arrange mushrooms and shrimp over fish. Pour sauce over all and top with grated cheese. Bake until heated through and cheese has melted, about 20 min.

Bake: 205° (400°)
Time: 10 min. + 20
Serves: 6

Arroz con Pollo

M.	Imp.	
1 3/4 Kg	4-lb	chicken pieces
5 ml	1t	salt
2ml	1/2t	pepper
.5 ml	1/8t	paprika
60 ml	1/4c	oil
1	1	minced garlic clove
1	1	chopped onion
450ml	2c	water
700 ml	3c	tomatoes
2	2	chicken bouillon cubes
1 ml	1/4t	powdered saffron
1	1	bay leaf
2 ml	1/2t	oregano or basil
450 ml	2c	uncooked rice
285 g	1-10 oz	package frozen peas

Season chicken with salt, pepper and paprika; brown in the hot oil. Place chicken in a large casserole. Sauté onion in remaining oil, add garlic, water, tomatoes, bouillon and seasonings. Bring to a boil; pour over chicken. Add rice and stir in. Cover tightly and bake 35 min. Uncover, toss rice and stir in the peas. Bake a further 15 min.

Bake: 180° (350°)
Time: 50
Serves: 6

Chicken Supreme

M.	Imp.	
284 ml	1 - 10 oz	can cream of mushroom soup
1	1	soup can milk
175 ml	3/4 c	raw rice
285 ml	1 - 10 oz	can sliced mushrooms
1	1	package onion soup mix
1	1	frying chicken, cut up

Mix soup and milk. Set half of mixture aside. Add rice, mushrooms and half package of onion soup to remaining soup. Place in a greased rectangular casserole. Place chicken pieces on top. Pour reserved soup mixture and remaining onion soup mix over top. Cover and bake 1 hour; uncover and bake a further 15 min.

Bake: 180° (350°)
Time: 1 hr + 15 min
Serves: 6

Rosita's Chicken Casserole

An unusual combination of flavors makes a most interesting dish

M	Imp	
1½ kg	3-lb	chicken pieces
175 ml	¾ c	flour
		salt and pepper
15 ml	3-4t	paprika
175 ml	¾ c	toasted slivered almonds
2	2	onions, sliced
284 ml	1-10 oz	can beef consommé
1	1	soup can of water
30 ml	2T	catsup
225 ml	1c	sour cream
6	6	peach halves
		grated Parmesan cheese

Coat chicken in the flour seasoned with salt, pepper and paprika. Brown the chicken pieces in bacon drippings, butter or oil and place in a shallow casserole. In remaining drippings lightly brown the onion slices and place over chicken along with the almonds. With any remaining seasoned flour make a mixture with the consommé, water, catsup and sour cream; pour over chicken. Bake covered 40 min. Uncover; top with peaches and cheese and bake a further 10 min.

Bake: 180° (350°)
Time: 50 min
Serves: 6

Chicken Bake Deluxe

M.	Imp.	
1½ kg	3-lb	chicken pieces, skinned
		bacon slices
450 ml	2 c	fresh sliced mushrooms
60 ml	¼ c	butter
2 ml	½ t	salt
60 ml	¼ c	flour
175 ml	¾ c	chicken broth
60 ml	¼ c	dry white wine
125 ml	½ c	whip cream

Roll one slice of bacon around each piece of chicken; secure with a toothpick. Place in a greased shallow casserole. Cover and bake for 1 hour; basting occasionally with the drippings. Meanwhile sauté the mushrooms in the butter. Place over cooked chicken and bake 15 min. uncovered. Make a sauce of any remaining drippings, salt, flour, broth, wine; stirring until thickened. Stir in cream and pour over casserole. Place under broiler until bubbly.

Bake: 200° (400°)
Time: 1 hr + 15 min
Serves: 4-6

Chicken Strata Supreme

M.	Imp.	
4	4	slices bread
450 ml	2 c	diced cooked chicken
60 ml	1/4 c	mayonnaise
125 ml	1/2 c	sliced mushrooms
30 ml	2 T	chopped pimiento
4	4	slices process cheese
284 ml	1 - 10 oz	can cream of mushroom soup
225 ml	1 c	milk
2	2	eggs
15 ml	1 T	parsley flakes
225 ml	1 c	bread crumbs
30 ml	2 T	melted margarine

Arrange bread slices in a square baking dish. Cover evenly with chicken; dot with mayonnaise; top with mushrooms and pimiento. Cover with cheese slices. Combine soup, milk, eggs and pour over chicken. Cover and refrigerate 2 hr or overnight. Combine bread crumbs, parsley flakes and margarine; sprinkle over top.

Bake: 180° (350°)
Time: 1 hr
Serves: 4

Baked Chicken with Cheese Sauce

M.	Imp.	
1½ kg	3 lb	frying chicken pieces
60 ml	¼ c	flour
125 ml	½ c	light cream
250 ml	1 c	grated cheese
284 ml	1-10 oz	can cream of mushroom soup
2 ml	½ t	salt
1 ml	¼ t	pepper
285 g	1-10 oz	package frozen peas and onions
125 ml	1 c	sliced mushrooms
2 ml	½ t	paprika

Coat chicken pieces with flour. Arrange, skin side down in a shallow casserole. Bake 205° (400°) 30 min. Turn and bake a further 20 min. Remove chicken from oven; drain off fat. Combine cream, cheese and soup add salt and pepper. Add peas, onions and mushrooms to chicken; pour sauce over all. Sprinkle with paprika. Cover and bake 20 min. at 160° (325°)

Bake: 205° (400°)
Time: 50 min
Bake: 160° (325°)
Time: 20 min.
Serves: 6

Chicken Fricasseé with Dumplings

M.	Imp.	
60 ml	1/4 c	flour
5 ml	1 t	salt
f.g.	f.g.	pepper
1 1/2 kg	3-lb	chicken pieces
30 ml	2 T	margarine
15 ml	1 T	chopped onion
1	1	grated carrot
5 ml	1 t	salt
1 ml	1/4 t	thyme
2 ml	1/2 t	marjoram
2 ml	1/2 t	rosemary
1	1	bay leaf
15 ml	1 T	parsley flakes
700 ml	3 c	chicken stock and water combined
450 ml	2 c	biscuit mix
2	2	beaten eggs
60 ml	1/4 c	milk

Coat chicken in the flour, salt and pepper. Brown chicken in the melted margarine. Add onion, carrot and seasonings stock and water. Cover and simmer gently 30 min. Combine biscuit mix, eggs and milk; drop by tablespoons over chicken and cover again for 15 min. Serve immediately.

Serves: 6

Chicken Divan

M.	Imp.	
1	1	large bunch broccoli
700 ml	3 c	cubed cooked chicken
60 ml	1/4 c	margarine
60 ml	1/4 c	flour
450 ml	2 c	chicken stock
125 ml	1/2 c	whip cream
45 ml	3 T	sherry (optional)
		salt and pepper to taste
		grated cheese

Peel and trim broccoli. Cut into stalks. Cook in salted water just until tender; drain. Arrange spears in a shallow casserole with flowerets to the outside. Melt margarine; blend in flour. Gradually add stock, stirring constantly. Fold in whipped cream, sherry and seasonings. Pour a little of the sauce over the broccoli. Arrange chicken down the centre and pour over remaining sauce. Sprinkle grated cheese over top and bake until heated through.

Bake: 180° (350°)
Time: 20 min.
Serves: 6

Chicken Tetrazzini

Cooked chicken baked with spaghetti in a rich cream sauce

M	Imp	
1 ℓ	4 c	diced cooked chicken
225 g	8 oz	thin spaghetti, cooked
125 ml	½ c	margarine
125 ml	½ c	flour
5 ml	1 t	salt
dash	dash	nutmeg, cayenne
450 ml	2 c	milk
225 ml	1 c	chicken broth
2	2	egg yolks
125 ml	½ c	cream
60 ml	¼ c	sherry
450 ml	2 c	fresh sliced mushrooms
30 ml	2 T	margarine
225 ml	1 c	grated cheddar cheese

Make a sauce of the 125 ml (½ c) margarine, flour, salt, nutmeg, cayenne, milk and broth. Beat egg yolks and cream; add a little hot sauce and return to saucepan; cook over low heat (do not boil) Remove from heat; add sherry. Sauté mushrooms until tender. Toss 225 ml (1 c) sauce with spaghetti; turn into a baking dish. Arrange chicken and mushroom over top Pour remaining sauce over. Sprinkle with cheese; bake.

Bake: 180° (350°)
Time: 30-45 min
Serves: 6

Chicken on a Bed of Rice

M.	Imp.	
125 ml	1/2 c	wild rice
250 ml	1 c	white rice
285 ml	1-10 oz	can whole mushrooms
175 ml	3/4 c	orange juice
		water
5 ml	1 t	salt
6	6	slices bacon, diced
6	6	carrots, peeled, quartered
1 1/2 kg	3-lb	chicken pieces
30 ml	2 T	flour
		salt and pepper to taste
1	1	minced garlic clove
60 ml	1/4 c	snipped fresh parsley

Place rice, drained mushrooms in a large casserole. Measure mushroom juice, orange juice and add sufficient water to make 750 ml (3c). Add to rice; add salt. Fry bacon until crisp; spread over rice. Layer carrots over top. Coat chicken with seasoned flour; brown in bacon dripping with garlic added. Place chicken over casserole; cover and bake until done. Remove chicken pieces; stir in parsley; replace chicken pieces and serve.

Bake: 205° (400°)
Time: 1 hr
Serves: 6

Coq au Vin

This makes an excellent do-ahead. Reheating only improves what is already delicious

M.	Imp.	
6	6	slices bacon cut up
60 ml	1/4 c	flour
2 ml	1/2 t	salt
1 ml	1/4 t	pepper
1	1	large frying chicken cut up
6	6	small onions
450 ml	2 c	sliced fresh mushrooms
284 ml	1 - 10 oz	can chicken broth
225 ml	1 c	red Burgondy wine
1	1	minced garlic clove
2 ml	1/2 t	salt
2 ml	1/2 t	thyme
1	1	bay leaf
30 ml	2 T	snipped parsley
4	4	carrots quartered
6	6	small potatoes

Coq au Vin (cont'd)

In a large skillet fry bacon just until crisp; remove. In the same skillet brown the chicken pieces that have been coated in the combined flour, salt and pepper. Place chicken and bacon in a large casserole.

Brown the mushrooms and whole onions in the skillet and add to casserole along with remaining ingredients. Bake, covered until chicken is tender and vegetables are done. Juices may be thickened if desired. Sprinkle with additional snipped parsley if desired.

Bake: 180° (350°)
Time: 1½ hr
Serves: 4-6

Cassoulet

A speedy version of the famous French provincial dish

M.	Imp.	
4	4	slices bacon, chopped
900 g	2 - lb	chicken pieces
450 g	1 - lb	lean boneless pork
450 g	1 - lb	lean boneless lamb
225 g	½ - lb	Italian sausage cut in 2 cm (1") slices
225 ml	1 c	onions, chopped
125 ml	½ c	celery, chopped
2	2	minced garlic cloves
450 ml	2 c	tomato sauce
225 ml	1 c	dry white wine
1	1	bay leaf
2 ml	½ t	thyme
700 ml	3 c	red kidney beans, canned
700 ml	3 c	white kidney beans, canned
		salt and pepper to taste
60 ml	¼ c	snipped parsley

Cassoulet (cont'd)

Cook bacon until nearly crisp; set aside. In the drippings brown chicken, pork, lamb and sausage; transfer to a large casserole. In the same pan, stir and cook onions, celery and garlic. Add tomato sauce, wine, bay leaf, thyme. Pour over meats and bake 1½.

Remove meats and to the sauce add the beans, combine well. Return meats and gently stir in. Top with bacon and bake a further hour. Sprinkle with parsley before serving.

<u>Variations</u>

- goose, duck or mutton may also be added or may replace one of the other meats
- you may use dried beans • cover with water and soak overnight. Drain; cover with fresh water and simmer 1-1¼ hr.
- may be made the day before and reheated
- top with buttered bread crumbs for the last 20 minutes of baking

Bake: 180° (350°)
Time: 2½ hr
Serves: 8

Chicken Sandwich Casserole

M.	Imp.	
12	12	slices bread, crusts removed
60 ml	1/4 c	softened margarine
10 ml	2 t	prepared mustard
450 ml	2 c	chopped cooked chicken
225 ml	1 c	grated cheese
284 ml	1-10 oz	can cream of chicken soup
285 g	1-10 oz	package frozen peas, thawed

Blend margarine and mustard and spread on one side of the bread slices. Arrange half of bread in one layer in a shallow casserole, buttered side up. Place chicken over bread and top with remaining bread slices. Combine soup and peas and spread evenly over sandwiches. Bake until heated through.

Bake: 180° (350°)
Time: 30 min
Serves: 6

Busy Day Casserole

An excellent dish with the simplest of preparations

M.	Imp.	
1 kg	2¼ lb	lean stewing beef, cubed
1	1	envelope dry onion soup mix
284 ml	1-10 oz	cream of mushroom soup
125 ml	½ c	red wine
2	2	chopped onions

Place all ingredients in a tightly covered casserole and bake.

Variation

- meatballs can be used in many recipes that call for stewing beef or cubed beef. Try them in savoury Beef Dish, Beef Imperial, Beef en Casserole as well as this Busy Day Casserole. Browning meatballs well before placing them in a casserole helps them to keep their shape.

Bake: 180° (350°)
Time: 2 hr
Serves: 6

Savoury Beef Dish

M.	Imp.	
1 kg.	2 lb	trimmed stewing beef
1 kg.	2 lb	peeled, sliced potatoes
500g	1 lb	peeled, sliced onions
500ml	2 c	beef stock
250 ml	1 c	red cooking wine
		salt
		pepper

Place all ingrediants in a covered casserole. Bake in a slow oven until done. Adjust seasoning if necessary. Juices may be thickened if desired using 25 ml. (1½ T.) flour per 250 ml. (1 cup) liquid.

Bake: 150°C (300°)
Time: 2½ hr
Serves: 4-6

Beef Imperial

The meat portion of this dish can be made well ahead of time and refrigerated or frozen until needed. Increase baking time accordingly.

M.	Imp.	
60 ml	1/4 c	flour
5 ml	1 t	salt
1 ml	1/4 t	pepper
450 g.	1-lb	boneless beef, cubed
225 ml	1 c	water
284 ml	1-10 oz	can cream of mushroom soup
30 ml	2 T	catsup
9-12	9-12	small boiled onions - fresh or canned
450 ml	2 c	mashed potatoes
15 ml	1 T	melted butter
1	1	egg

Coat meat in the flour seasoned with salt and pepper; brown in hot shortening. Add water and simmer until tender. (Pressure cooker saves time here) Stir in soup, catsup and onions; place in a deep casserole. Combine mashed potatoes, butter and egg; drop by spoonfuls over casserole and bake.

Bake: 180° (350°)
Time: 25 min
Serves: 4-6

Boeuf Bourguignon

Beef stew in red wine with bacon, onions and mushrooms

M.	Imp.	
4	4	slices bacon, diced
4	4	medium onions, sliced
450 ml	2 c	fresh sliced mushrooms
1 kg	2-lb	round steak, cubed
5 ml	1 t	salt
1 ml	1/4 t	marjoram
1 ml	1/4 t	thyme
f.g.	f.g.	pepper
25 ml	1 1/2 T	flour
175 ml	3/4 c	beef bouillon
350 ml	1 1/2 c	red Burgundy wine

Fry bacon in a skillet and remove. Cook onions and mushrooms in the bacon drippings and remove. Brown meat in the drippings; season with salt and pepper. Place bacon, meat, marjoram and thyme in a large casserole. To any remaining bacon drippings add bouillon, flour and heat, stirring until thickened. Add the Burgundy. Pour over meat and bake, covered 1 1/2 hr. Add onions and mushrooms and bake 30 min. uncovered.

Bake: 180° (350°)
Time: 2 hr
Serves: 6

My Favourite Stroganoff

M.	Imp.	
45 ml	3T	flour
5 ml	1t	salt
		pepper to taste
675 g	1½-lb	sirloin steak sliced into 5 cm (2") strips
30 ml	2T	oil
60 ml	4T	butter
125 ml	½c	sliced onions
1	1	minced garlic clove
450 ml	2 c	fresh sliced mushrooms
125 ml	½c	sherry
125 ml	½c	beef bouillon
5 ml	1t	chervil and/or parsley
15 ml	1T	lemon juice
2 ml	½t	paprika
225 ml	1 c	sour cream or yogurt

Dredge meat slices in seasoned flour. Heat oil and half the butter and brown meat (meat should still be rare); remove and keep warm. Add remaining butter to skillet with onions, garlic and mushrooms; cook 3 min. with stirring. Return meat, add sherry, bouillon, chervil, parsley, lemon paprika and additional salt and pepper if needed. Simmer 5 min. Stir in sour cream and heat through without boiling

Serves: 6

My Mom's Chile con Carne

M.	Imp.	
450 g	1-lb	ground beef
1	1	minced garlic clove
1	1	chopped onion
1/2	1/2	green pepper chopped
5 ml	1 t	salt
425 ml	1-15 oz	can red kidney beans
225 ml	1 c	tomato sauce
225 ml	1 c	tomato paste
5-10 ml	1-2 t	chili powder

Brown ground beef; add garlic, onion, green pepper, cook until tender. Add remaining ingredients and simmer 30 min.

Time: 30
Serves: 4

Beef en Casserole

M.	Imp.	
675 g	1½-lb	well trimmed stew beef
15 ml	1T	oil
		salt and pepper to taste
60 ml	¼c	brandy (optional)
12	12	small onions
6	6	carrots, quartered
225 ml	1c	mushrooms, quartered
15 ml	1T	steak sauce
45 ml	3T	tomato sauce
125 ml	½c	red wine
350 ml	1½c	beef broth
1	1	bay leaf
45 ml	3T	flour

Brown meat in hot oil. Heat brandy ignite it and add to the meat. Remove the meat to a casserole. Add the onions, carrots, mushrooms to the meat. Make a gravy of the steak sauce, tomato sauce, wine, broth and flour. Add bay leaf and pour all over the meat and vegetables.

Bake: 180° (350°)
Time: 1½ hr
Serves: 6

Pot-au-Feu

This can become a two-course meal; first the broth followed by the meat and vegetables or a delicious one course soup-stew.

M.	Imp.	
1800g	4-lb	lean short ribs
3	3	stalks celery with tops
1	1	onion studded with:
4	4	cloves
2	2	carrots
1	1	leek
1	1	bouquet garni of:

1 parsley sprig
1 bay leaf
1 clove garlic
6 peppercorns

Vegetable Garnish

3	3	carrots
3	3	stalks celery
3	3	leeks
4	4	potatoes
1/2	1/2	small cabbage
7 ml	1 1/2 t	salt

Pot-au-Feu (cont'd)

Place meat, celery, clored onion, carrot, leek and bouquet garni in a large pot. Cover with water and simmer until tender, about 2 hours. Set meat aside and strain vegetables (vegetables can be used in another soup recipe later). Skim off fat if necessary

Peel and quarter carrots; trim celery and cut into large pieces; wash leeks thoroughly and cut up; peel and quarter potatoes; trim cabbage and chop coarsely. Place meat, broth and prepared vegetables in a stove-top casserole dish and simmer until vegetables are just tender, about 45 min.

Time: 2 hr + 45 min
Serves: 6

Carbonnades à La Flamande

A famous Belgium stew of beef and onions braised in beer.

M.	Imp.	
1½ kg	3-lb	lean beef cubed
60 ml	¼ c	bacon fat
4-6	4-6	large onions, sliced
		salt and pepper to taste
2	2	minced garlic cloves
2-350 ml	2-12 oz	bottles beer
225 ml	1 c	beef bouillon
30 ml	2T	brown sugar
1	1	bay leaf
2 ml	½ t	thyme
15 ml	1T	parsley
30 ml	2T	cornstarch

Brown meat in hot bacon fat; transfer to a casserole. Brown onions lightly for 10 min. Stir in salt, pepper and garlic; add to meat. Add beer and bouillon and water (if needed) to barely cover meat. Add brown sugar, bay leaf, thyme and parsley. Bake 1½ hr. Mix cornstarch and a little water, stir into casserole. Return to oven for 15 min; stirring once or twice.

Bake: 160° (325°)
Time: 1 ¾ hr
Serves: 6

Carbonnades à La Flamande (cont'd)

Variations

• Classic Carbonnades à la Flammande·
about 15 min. before serving fat is skimmed and poured onto squares of stale bread. These are then spread with prepared mustard, generously and replaced on top of casserole and pushed into liquid. Bake uncovered 15 min to brown.

• Meatballs à La Flammande•
substitute meatballs for cubed beef. Reduce baking time to 1¼ hr

• Flemish stew • add peeled and quartered potatoes and carrots to the casserole

Six Layer Dinner

M.	Imp.	
3	3	medium potatoes, peeled and sliced
340 ml	1 - 12 oz	can kernel corn
1	1	onion sliced
450 g	1 - lb	ground beef
225 ml	1 c	sliced carrots
7 ml	1½ t	salt
		pepper to taste
450 ml	2 c	canned tomatoes

Layer potatoes, corn, onion, beef and carrots in a large casserole, seasoning each layer with salt and pepper. Pour tomatoes over all and bake.

Variations

- green beans may replace carrots or may be added as an additional vegetable
- substitute slightly diluted tomato soup or tomato sauce for the canned tomatoes
- add 80 ml (⅓ c) uncooked rice over the potato layer

Bake: 180° (350°)
Time: 1½ hr
Serves: 6

Cheesy Beef and Macaroni

M.	Imp.	
450 g	1-lb	ground beef
1	1	chopped onion
450 ml	2 c	tomato sauce
		salt and pepper to taste
225 ml	1 c	macaroni or other pasta
225 ml	1 c	grated cheddar cheese
60 ml	1/4 c	grated Parmesan cheese

Cook beef and onion together; drain if necessary. Add tomato sauce, salt and pepper and simmer gently for 5 min. Cook the macaroni. Place half of meat mixture in a casserole, then the macaroni and lastly, the remaining meat. Sprinkle cheeses over all and bake uncovered until heated through and cheese forms a crust.

Bake: 220° (425°)
Time: 25 min
Serves: 4

Jiffy Stroganoff

M.	Imp.	
450 g	1-lb	ground beef
1	1	package onion soup mix
2 ml	½ t	ginger
700 ml	3 c	noodles, uncooked
284 ml	1-10 oz	can sliced mushrooms
700-800 ml	3-3½ c	water
30 ml	2T	flour
225 ml	1 c	sour cream or yogurt
30 ml	2T	sherry

In an electric skillet, brown meat and drain if necessary. Sprinkle onion soup and ginger over top. Layer noodles over all; add mushrooms, undrained. Pour water over all and cover. Simmer 20-25 min. or until noodles are done. Combine flour and sour cream and stir into meat mixture. Cook 3 min longer; stir in sherry.

Time: 25 min
Serves: 4-6

Mock Chow Main Casserole

Quick and tasty this makes an easy family meal and a great contribution to any pot luck gathering

M.	Imp.	
450g.	1-lb	ground beef
1	1	onion, chopped
284 ml	1-10 oz	can cream of mushroom soup
800 ml	3½ c	water
350 ml	1½ c	diced celery
125 ml	½ c	rice uncooked
60 ml	4 T	soy sauce
284 ml	1-10 oz	can sliced mushrooms

Brown the ground beef and cook onions in the drippings. Combine with remaining ingredients in a greased casserole and bake with occasional stirring.

Bake: 180° (350°)
Time: 1½ hr
Serves: 6

Scalloped Beef and Potatoes

M.	Imp.	
4	4	potatoes, peeled and sliced
2	2	onions, sliced
450 g	1 - lb	ground beef
450 ml	2 c	meatless spaghetti sauce
15 ml	1 T	brown sugar
60 ml	1/4 c	grated cheese
60 ml	1/4 c	crushed cereal flakes or bread crumbs

Layer in a shallow casserole the potatoes, onions and ground beef. Combine the spaghetti sauce and brown sugar and pour over. Bake 40 min. covered. Combine cheese and crumbs for a topping and bake a further 30 min uncovered.

Bake: 180° (350°)
Time: 70 min
Serves: 4

Lazy-Day Lasagne

Similar to lasagne but with much less effort

M.	Imp.	
225 g	8 oz	wide uncooked noodles
450 g	1-lb	ground beef
450 ml	2 c	tomato sauce
2 ml	1/2 t	basil or oregano
225 ml	1 c	cottage cheese
60 ml	1/4 c	sour cream
30 ml	2 T	parsley flakes
2 ml	1/2 t	salt

Cook noodles in boiling salted water and drain. Cook and stir meat in a large skillet; drain. Add tomato sauce and basil and heat through. Mix cottage cheese, sour cream, parsley and salt. Layer half of noodles in a casserole, then cheese and then remaining noodles. Pour meat mixture evenly over top.

Bake: 180° (350°)
Time: 40
Serves: 4-6

My Favourite Lasagne

M.	Imp.	
450 g	1 - lb	ground beef
1	1	minced garlic clove
15 ml	1 T	basil
5 ml	1 t	salt
450 ml	2 c	tomatoes
325 ml	1 1/3 c	tomato paste
8-10	8-10	lasagne noodles
700 ml	3 c	cottage cheese
125 ml	1/2 c	grated Parmesan cheese
30 ml	2 T	parsley flakes
2	2	eggs
7 ml	1 1/2 t	salt
450 g	1 - lb	sliced Mozzarella cheese

Brown meat; drain off excess fat. Add garlic, basil, salt, tomatoes and tomato paste. Simmer 30 min.

Cook enough lasagne noodles to make two layers in the casserole dish plus along sides for borders.

Combine cottage cheese, Parmesan, parsley, eggs and salt.

Place half of noodles in casserole, spread with half of cottage cheese

My Favourite Lasagne (cont'd)

filling, half of Mozzarella, half of meat sauce. Repeat layers. Bake and let stand 10 min. before serving.

Variations

• One-step Lasagne • add 125 ml (1/2 c) water to meat sauce. Spread a third of meat sauce in casserole then uncooked lasagne noodles, continue as above. Increase cooking time to 50 min.

• Meatless Lasagne • omit meat; add sautéed onions and mushrooms to the tomato sauce; continue same as above

• Spinach Lasagne • omit meat; cook, drain and chop 450 g (1-lb) spinach. Blend into tomato sauce and continue as above

Bake: 190° (375°)
Time: 30
Serves: 12

Pastitio

A very popular Greek dish

M.	Imp.	
225 ml	1c	elbow macaroni, cooked and drained
450 g	1-lb	ground beef
1	1	large onion, chopped
450 ml	2 c	tomato purée
5 ml	1t	salt
5 ml	1t	cinnamon
225 ml	1c	cottage cheese
1	1	egg

Rich Cheese Sauce

60 ml	1/4c	margarine
60 ml	1/4c	flour
5 ml	1t	chicken flavoring
425 ml	1-15 oz	can evaporated milk
125 ml	1/2c	water
125 ml	1/2c	grated Parmesan cheese

Pastitio (cont'd)

Brown ground beef and sauté onions in the drippings. Drain off excess fat if necessary. Stir in purée, salt and cinnamon. Simmer 15 min.

Combine macaroni, cottage cheese and egg; line a large pie plate with the mixture. Pour the meat mixture into the macaroni shell. Top with a portion of the Rich Cheese Sauce and sprinkle with additional Parmesan cheese. Bake and serve with remaining Cheese Sauce

To prepare Rich Cheese Sauce:

Melt margarine, add flour gradually; add seasonings. Gradually add milk and water; stir until thickened. Stir in cheese.

Bake: 190° (375°)
Time: 30 min
Serves: 6

Pork Casserole

Especially good served with fettucine verde - 'green' egg noodles

M.	Imp.	
675-900 g	1 1/2 - 2 lb	lean pork, cubed
60 ml	1/4 c	bacon fat
225 ml	1 c	chopped onion
1/2	1/2	lemon juiced
1	1	bay leaf
5 ml	1 t	salt
225 ml	1 c	red wine
125 ml	1/2 c	flour
125 ml	1/2 c	water
1	1	chicken bouillon cube
225 ml	1 c	fresh sliced mushrooms
1	1	minced garlic clove
30 ml	2 T	margarine
75 ml	1/3 c	white wine
350 ml	1 1/2 c	sour cream

Brown meat in hot bacon fat. Transfer to a casserole. Fry onions for 5 min.; add to meat. Add lemon, bay leaf, salt and half of red wine. Bake 30 min. Make a sauce of the flour, water, bouillon and remaining red wine; stir into meat. Sauté mushrooms and garlic in the margarine; add white wine and simmer 5 min. Add to meat and bake 30 min. Stir in sour cream and heat through; about 10 min.

Bake: 180° (350°)

Time: 1 hr 10 min

Serves: 6

Veal Casserole

Lean stewing beef can be substituted when veal is scarce

M.	Imp.	
4	4	slices bacon, cut 2.5 cm (1")
1½ kg	3-lb	veal cut in large cubes
350 ml	1½ c	sliced onion
225 ml	1 c	dry white wine or vermouth
450-700 ml	2-3 c	beef stock or beef bouillon
		salt and pepper to taste
2	2	minced garlic cloves
2 ml	½ t	thyme
1	1	bay leaf
350 ml	1½ c	diced tomatoes
225 ml	1 c	rice
225 ml	1 c	grated Swiss cheese

Brown bacon and place in a casserole. Brown meat in the drippings and add to bacon. Brown onions lightly; add to meats. Add wine to skillet to scrape up juices; pour over meats. Add bouillon, salt, pepper, garlic, thyme and bay leaf. Bake 1½ hr. Add tomatoes, rice and bake a further 1½ hr. Gently stir in cheese just before serving

Bake: 180° (350°)
Time: 3 hr
Serves: 6

Stuffed Manicotti

Giant pasta stuffed with cheeses

M.	Imp.	
450 g	1-lb	ground beef, browned, drained
1	1	chopped onion
1	1	minced garlic clove
325 ml	1 1/3 c	tomato paste
450 ml	2 c	water
30 ml	2 T	parsley flakes
15 ml	1 T	basil
5 ml	1 t	salt
700 ml	3 c	cottage cheese
150 ml	2/3 c	grated Parmesan cheese
2	2	eggs
30 ml	2 T	parsley flakes
2 ml	1/2 t	salt
12	12	manicotti shells, cooked
175 ml	3/4	grated Parmesan cheese

Make a meat sauce of the meat, onion, garlic, tomato paste, water, parsley, basil and salt. Simmer 20 min. Combine cottage cheese, Parmesan, eggs, parsley and salt. Fill the manicotti shells. Pour half of meat sauce in casserole. Arrange manicotti over top. Top with remaining meat sauce and Parmesan

Bake: 180° (350°)
Time: 40 min
Serves: 6-8

Deep Dish Pizza

This is a simple quick version ready for your favorite toppings

M	Imp.	
225 g	1/2 lb	ground beef
225 ml	1 c	biscuit mix
60 ml	1/4 c	milk
5 ml	1 t	Italian seasoning divided
125 ml	1/2 c	tomato sauce
15 ml	1 T	finely chopped onion
2 ml	1/2 t	sugar
1 ml	1/4 t	garlic powder
225 ml	1 c	shredded mozzarella
		grated Parmesan cheese

Cook and stir ground beef in skillet until brown; drain. Stir biscuit mix and milk until blended. Knead on a lightly floured board 10 times; roll to fit a pie plate. Mix half of the Italian seasoning, tomato sauce, onion, sugar and garlic powder. Spread evenly on crust. Layer meat over top then mozzarella cheese. Sprinkle with remaining Italian seasoning and Parmesan.

Bake: 220°(425°)
Time: 15-20
Serves: 4

Easy-out 'Cabbage Rolls'

M.	Imp.	
675 g	1½-lb	ground beef
2	2	medium onions, chopped
1	1	minced garlic clove
5 ml	1 t	salt
		pepper to taste
450 ml	2c	tomato sauce
225 ml	1 c	water
125 ml	½c	rice
450 ml	4 c	shredded cabbage

Cook and stir meat until brown; stir onion, garlic, salt and pepper. Add tomato sauce, rice and water. Simmer 20 min. (rice will not be completely cooked) Place half of cabbage in a casserole. Top with half of meat mixture. Repeat layers and bake.

Variation

• using same quantities as above make layers of half the cabbage, rice, onions, meat seasonings and cabbage. Combine tomato sauce and water and pour over. Increase baking time to 1½ hr

Bake: 180° (350°)
Time: 1 hr
Serves: 6

Saturday Night Casserole

This casserole was often served along with Hockey Night in Canada! We enjoyed it as young children and now as adults

M.	Imp.	
450 g	1-lb	ground beef
1	1	large onion chopped
450 ml	2 c	canned tomatoes
225 ml	1 c	rice
		salt and pepper to taste

Brown meat and onion; drain off excess fat if necessary. Stir in tomatoes and seasonings. Cook rice in 450 ml (2c) salted water. Put meat mixture in a deep casserole. Top with rice. Cover and bake

Bake: 180° (350°)
Time: 40 min
Serves: 4-6

Wild Rice and Sausage

M.	Imp.	
450 g.	1-lb	bulk pork sausage or ground pork
125 ml	1/2 c	chopped celery
15 ml	1 T	chopped green pepper and/ or pimiento
284 ml	1-10 oz	can mushroom soup
225 ml	1 c	hot water
175 ml	3/4 c	wild rice or a combination of wild rice plus white rice
175 ml	3/4 c	grated cheese
125 ml	1/2 c	sliced mushrooms
15 ml	1 T	minced onion
1	1	chicken bouillon cube
2 ml	1/2 t	marjoram
2 ml	1/2 t	thyme

Brown meat; add celary, green pepper, cook 5 min. and drain. Add remaining ingrediants, mix thorougnly and bake until liquid is absorbed and rice is tender.

Bake: 170° (325°)
Time: 1½ hr
Serves: 6-8

Seven Layer Sausage Dinner

M.	Imp.	
4	4	potatoes, peeled, sliced
2	2	onions, sliced
60 ml	1/4 c	rice
4	4	carrots, peeled, sliced
285 g	1-10 oz	package frozen peas
450 g	1-lb	sausage links
284 ml	1-10 oz	can tomato soup
225 ml	1 c	water

Layer potatoes, onions, rice, carrots and peas in a deep casserole. Arrange sausage links spoke fashion over top. Combine soup and water; pour over all. Bake covered 1 hr.; turn sausages and bake uncovered 1 hr.

Bake: 180° (350°)
Time: 2 hr
Serves: 6

Yankee Noodle Bake

M.	Imp.	
8	8	weiners, sliced
60 ml	1/4c	chopped onion
30 ml	2T	margarine
450 ml	2 c	cooked macaroni or noodles
284 ml	1-10 oz	can tomato soup
125 ml	1/2 c	water
5 ml	1t	prepared mustard
60 ml	1/4 c	bread crumbs
30 ml	2T	melted margarine

Gently fry weiners and onions in 30 ml (2T) margarine. Add tomato soup, water, mustard and stir until smooth. Pour over cooked macaroni and stir lightly to combine. Top with bread crumbs combined with 30 ml (2T) melted margarine. Bake until heated through.

Bake: 180° (350°)
Time: 30 min
Serves: 4

Pork Chop and Potato Scallop

M.	Imp.	
4	4	pork chops
4	4	medium potatoes, sliced
1/2	1/2	onion, thinly sliced
284 ml	1 - 10 oz	cream of mushroom soup
125 ml	1/2 c	sour cream
60 ml	1/4 c	water
15 ml	1 T	parsley flakes
175 ml	3/4 c	shredded cheese

Brown pork chops. Blend soup, sour cream, water, parsley and cheese. In a casserole alternate layers of potatoes and onions and sauce. Top with chops. Cover and bake.

Bake: 190° (375°)
Time: 1 1/4 hr
Serves: 4

Steak Soup

M.	Imp.	
450gm	1-lb	ground beef
250 ml	1 c	chopped onion
125 ml	½ c	chopped celery and/or green pepper
540 ml	1-19oz	can tomato juice
250 ml	1 c	grated carrot
1	1	beef bouillon cube
5 ml	1 t	seasoned salt
2 ml	½t	salt
f.g.	f.g.	pepper
250 ml	1 c	grated potato
30 ml	2 T	parsley flakes
75 ml	⅓ c	flour
1 l.	4 c	milk

In a large saucepan brown meat. Remove all but enough fat to sauté onion, celery and green pepper. Cook 5 min. Add tomato juice, vegetables and seasonings and simmer for 20 min. Combine flour and 225 ml (1 c.) of the milk; stir into soup. Stir until thickened. Add remaining milk and heat thoroughly. Adjust seasoning if necessary.

Serves: 8

Lentil Soup with Beef and Barley

M.	Imp.	
225 gm	1/2 lb	ground beef
250 ml	1 c	lentils
60 ml	1/4 c	barley
1.25 l	5-6 c	water or stock
284 ml	1-10 oz.	can beef broth
1	1	large onion, chopped
1	1	garlic clove, minced
1	1	large carrot, diced
1	1	celery stalk, diced
450 ml	2 c	canned tomatoes
1	1	bay leaf
pinch	pinch	thyme
pinch	pinch	basil

Sauté beef in a large saucepan. Drain off excess fat. Add remaining ingredients and simmer, covered until done, 1-1½ hr.

Serves: 8-10

Barley Burger Soup

M.	Imp.	
450gm	1 lb	ground beef
1	1	medium onion chopped
2	2	stalks celery chopped
1 l	4 c	tomato juice
225ml	1 c	water or more
10 ml	2t	salt
10-15 ml	2-3t	chili powder
		pepper to taste
125ml	1/4 c	barley

Cook and stir ground beef and onion in a large saucepan for 5 min. Drain off excess fat. Add remaining ingredients and simmer 1 hour. Adjust seasonings if necessary.

Serves: 4

Scotch Broth

The Stock

M.	Imp	
1½ kg	3-4 lb	lamb, meat and bones
2 ℓ	8 c	water
10 ml	2t	salt
15 ml	1T	seasoned salt
2	2	stalks celery with leaves
2ml	½t	thyme
6	6	peppercorns
2 ml	½t	cardamon
1	1	bay leaf

The Soup

60 ml	¼c	margarine
½	½	chopped onion
1	1	large carrot, diced
1	1	stalk celery, diced
125 ml	½c	barley
45 ml	3T	flour
2 ℓ	8 c	stock from above
225 ml	1 c	light cream

Combine stock ingredients; simmer 2 hours and strain. Set stock and meat pieces aside. Sauté soup vegetables in the margarine until tender. Add barley, meat from the stock and most of the stock. Add flour to reserved stock and stir into soup. Simmer 1 hour. Stir in cream; heat through.

Serves: 8

Frankfurter-Lentil Soup

M.	Imp.	
2	2	slices bacon, finely diced
1	1	stalk celery, diced
1	1	carrot, diced
1/2	1/2	onion, chopped
1	1	garlic clove, minced
2 ℓ	8 c	water
450 gm	1-lb	lentils
125 ml	1/2 c	diced canned tomatoes
1	1	bay leaf
4	4	large European frankfurters, sliced
15 ml	1T.	steak sauce
		salt and pepper to taste

Fry bacon and set aside. Sauté celery, carrot, onion, garlic for 4 min. in the drippings. Add water, lentils, tomatoes and bay leaf. Simmer, covered, 1 hour or until done. Add remaining ingredients and simmer a further 10 min.

Serves: 6

Minestrone

A thick and hearty soup that can manage any variety of vegetables

M.	Imp.	
2	2	slices bacon, diced
1	1	minced garlic clove
1	1	chopped onion
1	1	leek, diced
5 ml	1t	parsley flakes
5 ml	1t	basil
15 ml	1T	tomato paste
3	3	tomatoes, peeled, chopped
3	3	stalks celery, chopped
2	2	carrots, sliced
2	2	potatoes, diced
1/2	1/2	turnip, peeled, diced
1/4	1/4	cabbage, shredded
1	1	zucchini, sliced
2 ℓ	8c	water
		salt and pepper to taste
400 ml	1-19 oz	can kidney beans
250 ml	1c	elbow macaroni
		grated Parmesan cheese

Lightly cook bacon, garlic, onion, leek, parsley and basil. Add all but beans and macaroni; simmer 45 min. Add beans and macaroni and cook a further 10 min. Sprinkle with Parmesan cheese as a garnish

Serves: 8

Country Corn Chowder

M.	Imp.	
1	1	onion, chopped
1	1	celery stalk, diced
1	1	bay leaf
2 ml	1/2 t	basil
30 ml	2 T	margarine or bacon fat
225 ml	1 c	water
400 ml	1 - 14 oz.	can cream corn
325 ml	1 1/2 c	milk
225 ml	1 c	canned tomatoes
6	6	frankfurters, sliced
5 ml	1 t	salt
		pepper to taste
125 ml	1/2 c	shredded cheddar cheese
15 ml	1 T	parsley flakes

Cook onion, celery, bay leaf and basil in margarine or bacon fat 5 min. Add water and corn and simmer 10 min. Remove bay leaf. Add milk, tomatoes, frankfurters and seasonings. Heat through. Stir in cheese and parsley just before serving.

Serves: 6

Vegetable Soup

M.	Imp.	
1½ kg	3 lb	soup bones
2 l	2 qt	water
500 ml	2 c	tomatoes
1	1	large carrot, sliced
1	1	stalk celery, diced
2	2	medium potatoes, diced
340 ml	1-12 oz	can kernel corn
½	½	onion or leek, chopped
30 ml	2 T	seasoned salt
5 ml	1 t	celery salt
		pepper to taste
1 ml	¼ t	thyme
2 ml	½ t	savory
1	1	beef bouillon cube

Place all the ingredients in a large soup kettle and simmer gently for 3 hours. Remove bones and adjust seasonings.

Serves: 10

Quick Bean Soup

M.	Imp.	
3	3	slices diced bacon
450 ml	2 c	baked beans
284 ml	1-10 oz	can tomato soup
450 ml	2 c	chili with meat
300 ml	1 1/4 c	water
1	1	minced garlic clove

Fry bacon until crisp. Combine remaining ingredients in a saucepan; add crisped bacon and heat through. Good served with corn chips.

Serves: 4-6

Onion Soup Gourmet

A thick and hearty casserole of onions and cheese; a must for all onion soup lovers

M.	Imp.	
12	12	slices of French bread cut 1½ cm (½") thick
1 ℓ	4 c	onion soup (diluted canned onion soup is fine)
700 ml	3 c	grated mixed cheeses such as cheddar, swiss
60 ml	¼ c	red wine

Toast bread in the oven. Place half of the bread in one layer in a casserole. Top with half the cheese, half the soup. Repeat layers and pour wine over all. Bake until soup is all absorbed and cheese has browned.

Bake: 180° (350°)
Time: 1 hr
Serves: 4

Clam Chowder

M.	Imp.	
6	6	large potatoes
1	1	large onion, sliced
5	5	stalks celery, diced
800 ml	4c	tomatoes
2-285 ml	2-10 oz	cans baby clams, undrained

In a large saucepan cover potatoes with water and cook until overdone; mash. Add remaining ingredients and simmer 1 hour. Adjust seasonings if necessary.

Variations

- diced bacon may be added during the cooking period
- light cream may be added after cooking. Do not boil
- 60 ml (1/4c) or more of fresh snipped parsley adds flavor and interest

Serves: 8

Oven Fish Chowder

M.	Imp.	
900g	2-lb	cod fillets, cut up
4	4	medium potatoes, sliced
125 ml	½c	chopped celery leaves
½	½	large onion chopped
450 ml	2 c	water
30 ml	2T	margarine
125 ml	½c	white wine
10 ml	2t	salt
1	1	bay leaf
1	1	minced garlic clove
3	3	whole cloves
2 ml	½t	dill weed
dash	dash	white pepper
450 ml	2 c	light cream
		chopped parsley

Place fish, vegetables, water, margarine, wine and salt in a casserole. Make a spice bag of the bay leaf, garlic, cloves and dill weed. Add to casserole. Bake 1 hour. Scald cream and add to casserole. Garnish with chopped parsley.

Bake: 180° (350°)
Time: 1 hr.
Serves: 8

Fisherman's Chowder

M.	Imp.	
6	6	slices bacon, diced
1	1	small leek, sliced
450 ml	2 c	clam nectar or fish stock
700 ml	3 c	water
3	3	medium potatoes, cut up
2	2	medium carrots, diced
60 ml	1/4 c	flour
125 ml	1/2 c.	water
450 ml	2 c.	milk
1 kg	2 lb.	assorted fish such as cod, halibut, red snapper
100 g	1/4 lb.	shrimp
100 g	1/4 lb.	clams
285 g	1 - 10 oz	package frozen peas
1 ml	1/4 t	dill weed
7 ml	1 1/2 t	salt
1 ml	1/4 t	white pepper

In a large saucepan, sauté bacon lightly and set aside. In the drippings, sauté leek until tender - about 5 min. Stir in clam nectar, 700 ml (3 c) water and vegetables. Simmer until tender - about 15 min. Combine flour and the 125 ml (1/2 c) water and stir into soup. Stir until thickened. Stir in remaining ingredients and simmer until fish is tender - about 10 min

Serves: 10

Beggar's Bouillabaisse

M.	Imp.	
2-425gm	2-16oz	cans stewed tomatoes
475 ml	2-8oz	cans tomato sauce
2	2	medium potatoes, diced
1	1	medium onion, diced
1/2	1/2	green pepper, diced
2	2	minced garlic cloves
1	1	bay leaf
75 ml	1/4-1/2 c	freshly snipped parsley
5 ml	1t.	Italian herb seasoning
5 ml	1t.	salt
2 ml	1/2t.	ground white pepper
1 kg.	2 1/2 lb.	firm-flesh fish such as snapper, cod etc., cut into large bite-sized pieces
225gm	1/2 lb	shrimp
180gm	1-6oz	tin baby clams, undrained

Combine all the ingredients except the seafoods in a large sauce-pan. Simmer 30 minutes or until vegetables are tender. Add fish, shrimp and clams and simmer a further 10-15 min. Adjust seasonings.

Serves: 6-8

Fisherman's Wharf Cioppino

A speciality of San Francisco

M.	Imp	
2	2	onions, chopped
15 ml	1T	oil
2	2	minced garlic cloves
30ml	2T	snipped parsley
60 ml	1/4c	mixed vegetable juice
3	3	tomatoes, peeled, chopped (seeded if desired)
2 ml	1/2t	basil
675 g	1 1/2 lb	cod fillets cut into bite size pieces

Cook onion and garlic in the oil until tender. Simmer all the ingredients except fish for 30 min. Add fish and cook gently a further 10 min. or until fish is cooked.

Variations

Add any of the following to become a house speciality: green pepper, leeks, tomato juice, tomato purée, bay leaf, white wine, halibut, bass, oysters, lobster, crab, clam

Time: 40 min.
Serves: 4

Fancy Asparagus Casserole

M.	Imp.	
30 ml	2T	margarine
30 ml	2T	flour
125 ml	½ c	milk
400 ml	1 - 14 oz can	asparagus pieces
5 ml	1 t	salt
		pepper to taste
2 ml	½ t	celery salt
15 ml	1 T	lemon juice
5 ml	1 t	catsup
5 ml	1 t	worcestershire sauce
2 ml	½ t	prepared mustard
225 ml	1 c	shredded cheese
2	2	hard cooked eggs, chopped
125 ml	½ c	chopped almonds or pecans
60 ml	¼ c	bread crumbs
30 ml	2T	melted margarine

Make a sauce of 30 ml (2T) margarine, flour, milk, drained vegetable juice. Stir in salt, pepper, celery salt, lemon juice, catsup, worcestershire, mustard and cheese. Fold in asparagus pieces, eggs, almonds and pour into a greased casserole. Top with bread crumbs combined with 30 ml (2T) melted margarine.

Bake: 180° (350°)
Time: 30 min
Serves: 6

Broccoli Onion Deluxe

M.	Imp.	
2	2	medium bunches broccoli peeled and cut up
450 ml	2c	small whole onions
225 ml	1c	milk
30 ml	2T	flour
15 ml	1T	butter
1 ml	1/4t	salt
85 g	1-3 oz	package cream cheese
225 ml	1c	bread crumbs
30 ml	2T	melted butter
60 ml	1/4c	grated Parmesan cheese

Cook broccoli and onions separately, just until done. Make a white sauce of the milk, flour, butter and salt. Stir in the cream cheese. Pour the cheese sauce over the vegetables and bake 20 min. Combine the bread crumbs melted butter and Parmesan for a topping and bake a further 15 min.

Variation

- Brussels sprouts may replace the broccoli

Bake: 180° (350°)
Time: 35 min.
Serves : 10

Broccoli Casserole

M.	Imp.	
1	1	large bunch broccoli peeled and cut up
284 ml	1-10 oz	can cream of mushroom soup
150 ml	2/3 c	grated cheddar cheese
125 ml	1/2 c	mayonnaise
15 ml	1 T	fresh lemon juice
225 ml	1 c	bread crumbs
60 ml	1/4 c	slivered almonds, toasted

Cook broccoli just until tender; combine with mushroom soup, cheese, mayonnaise and lemon juice. Place in a casserole and top with bread crumbs and almonds.

Variations

- replace a portion of the broccoli with cauliflower, zucchini and lightly sautéed mushrooms
- add a small amount of diced pimientos for a splash of color

Bake: 180° (350°)
Time: 20 min.
Serves: 6

Creole Bean and Cheese Casserole

M.	Imp.	
75 ml	1/3 c	chopped onion
30 ml	2 T	margarine
550 ml	2 1/2 c	canned tomatoes
5 ml	1 t	chili powder
5 ml	1 t	salt
225 ml	1 c	soft bread cubes
285 g.	1 - 10 oz	package frozen lima beans, cooked, drained
225 g.	1 - 8 oz	package process cheese slices

Sauté onion in margarine until tender. Add tomatoes, chili powder and salt. Simmer 10 min. Add bread and combine gently. Place half of the beans in a greased shallow casserole. Add half the tomato sauce, half the cheese Add remaining beans, tomato sauce and bake. Arrange remaining cheese slices over top and bake a further 5 min.

Bake: 180° (350°)
Time: 30 min.
Serves: 4-6

Green Bean Casserole

M.	Imp.	
700 ml	3 c	cooked green beans, French style or cut
284 ml	1 - 10 oz	can cream of mushroom soup
5 ml	1 t	soy sauce or worcestershire
85 g	1 - 3½ oz	can French fried onions

Stir soup and soy sauce until smooth; mix in beans and half of onions. Bake until bubbly. Top with remaining onions and bake another 5 min.

Bake: 180° (350°)
Time: 20 + 5 min
Serves: 6

Jane's Vegetable Casserole

M.	Imp.	
284 ml	1 - 10 oz	can cream of moshroom soup
250-350 ml	1 - 1½ c	grated cheese
450 ml	2 c	cooked rice: brown, white wild rice or a combination
1	1	large bunch broccoli, trimmed, cut up, cooked
125 ml	½ c	bread crumbs
30 ml	2 T	butter or margarine
60 ml	¼ c	grated cheese

Combine soup cheese, rice and broccoli. Place in a greased casserole. Top with bread crumbs; dot with butter; sprinkle with cheese

Bake: 180° (350°)
Time: 25 min
Serves: 6

Cauliflower Puff

M.	Imp.	
1	1	large cauliflower
45 ml	3T	margarine
45 ml	3T	flour
2 ml	1/2t	salt
350 ml	1 1/2 c	milk
175 ml	3/4 c	grated cheddar cheese
4	4	eggs, separated
5 ml	1 t	sugar
		paprika

Break cauliflower into flowerets and cook in salted water just until tender. Drain and place in a shallow buttered casserole. Make a white sauce of the margarine, flour, salt and milk and stir in grated cheese. Beat egg yolks, sugar and a f.g. salt and pepper and add to cheese sauce. Fold in stiffly beaten egg whites. Pour sauce over cauliflower; sprinkle with paprika and bake.

Bake: 180°(350°)
Time: 20 min
Serves: 6

West Coast Cauliflower

M.	Imp.	
1	1	head cauliflower
1-285 ml	1-10 oz	package frozen peas, cooked
284 ml	1-10 oz	can cream of shrimp soup
60 ml	1/4 c	milk
1 ml	1/4 t	salt
		pepper to taste
450 ml	2 c	cooked shrimp
60 ml	1/4 c	bread crumbs
30 ml	2 T	melted butter
30 ml	2 T	grated Parmesan cheese

Cook cauliflower whole in salted water just until tender. Drain and place in a casserole. Place cooked peas around cauliflower. Heat soup and milk together, stir in seasonings and shrimp. Heat through and pour over vegetables. Top with bread crumbs that have been tossed with melted butter and Parmesan cheese. Broil until lightly browned.

Broil
Time: 10 min
Serves: 6

Corn Casserole

M.	Imp.	
400 ml	1-14 oz	can cream corn
1	1	egg, beaten
175 ml	3/4 c	milk
150 ml	2/3 c	cracker crumbs
80 ml	5-6 T	grated cheddar cheese

Combine thoroughly, all ingredients in a well greased casserole. Bake until set.

Bake: 180° (350°)
Time: 40 min
Serves: 6

Country Kitchen Corn Ring

M.	Imp.	
250 ml	1 c	bread crumbs
30 ml	2 T	margarine, melted
398 ml	1-19 oz	can cream corn
2	2	eggs, beaten
60 ml	1/4 c	onion, chopped
2 ml	1/2 t	salt

Combine thoroughly, all ingredients in a well greased casserole or a ring mold. Unmold to serve and fill with another cooked vegetable.

Bake: 180° (350°)
Time: 45 min.
Servings: 6

Buffet Vegetable Bake

M.	Imp.	
2-285 g	2-10 oz	packages frozen peas and carrots
285 g	1-10 oz	package frozen cut green beans
140 ml	1-5 oz	can water chestnuts, drained and sliced
175 ml	3/4 c	sliced mushrooms, drained
284 ml	1-10 oz	can cream mushroom soup
45 ml	3 T	sherry
5 ml	1 t	worcestershire sauce
450 ml	2 c	shredded cheese
80 ml	1/3 c	cracker crumbs

Cook peas, carrots, beans just until tender; drain. Add water chestnuts and mushrooms. Combine mushroom soup sherry, worcestershire and cheese. Gently stir in vegetables and turn into a casserole. Bake, stirring occasionally. Sprinkle cracker crumbs over just before serving.

Bake: 180° (350°)
Time: 45 min
Serves: 10

Brown Rice and Vegetables

M.	Imp.	
575 ml	2 1/2 c	water
2	2	chicken bouillon cubes
225 ml	1 c	brown rice
1	1	bunch broccoli, peeled, cut
1	1	head cauliflower, broken
1	1	zucchini, sliced
2	2	stalks celery, sliced
250 ml	1 c	mushrooms sliced
1	1	small carrot grated
30-60 ml	2T	snipped chives
30-60 ml	2T	snipped parsley
2 ml	1/2 t	soy sauce
6	6	slices cheese such as cheddar, Swiss, jack)
45 ml	3T	roasted sunflower seeds

Cook the rice in the water and bouillon until tender, about 45 min. Remove from heat and uncover. Combine broccoli cauliflower, zucchini and celery and steam 10 min. Steam mushrooms for 2 min. Toss rice with grated carrot, chives and parsley. Add soy sauce. Place rice mixture in casserole; top with vegetables. Cover with cheese slices. Bake. Sprinkle with sunflower seeds before serving.

Bake: 180° (350°)
Time: 20 min.
Serves: 6

Baked Ratatouille

Equally delicious hot or cold

M.	Imp.	
2	2	large onions, sliced
2	2	minced garlic cloves
1	1	eggplant peeled, cubed
3	3	zucchini, cut in chunks
1	1	green pepper cut in chunks
4	4	tomatoes, cut up
7 ml	1½ t	salt
5 ml	1 t	basil
60 ml	¼ c	snipped parsley
5 ml	1 t	sugar
30 ml	2 T	olive oil
		grated Parmesan cheese

Layer the vegetables in a large casserole sprinkling the seasonings evenly throughout. Drizzle the olive oil over all and bake covered. Mix gently before serving and garnish generously with the Parmesan cheese.

Bake: 180° (350°)
Time: 1½ - 2 hr
Serves: 10

Oven Baked Rice and Variations

M.	Imp.	
225 ml	1 c	white rice
30 ml	2 T	margarine
60 ml	1/4 c	chopped onion
175 ml	3/4 c	water
225 ml	1 c	chicken broth
60-125 ml	1/4 - 1/2 c	white wine
2 ml	1/2 t	salt

Sauté onion in butter until tender. Add with remaining ingredients to a greased cassarole and bake until rice is tender and liquid is absorbed.

Variations

- use a combination of wild rice, brown rice and/or white rice
- Venetian rice • toss cooked rice with crisp diced bacon, peas and parmesan cheese
- Herbed rice • Sauté celery with the onion and continue as above. Toss cooked rice with snipped parsley and toasted pine nuts
- complement the main entrée by substituting beef broth, orange juice etc for water and chicken broth

Bake: 180° (350°)
Time: 45 min
Serves: 4

Spanakopita

A Greek spinach pie made with paper thin phyllo pastry

M	Imp.	
900 g	2 - lb	spinach
125 m	½ c	margarine
10	10	sheets phyllo pastry
225 g	½ lb	feta, cheddar or Gruyère cheese
125 g	1 c	cottage cheese
3	3	eggs, well beaten
		salt and pepper to taste
2 ml	½ t	nutmeg

Cook or steam spinach just until done; drain and chop. Brush half of phyllo sheets with melted margarine and lay in a shallow rectangular casserole. Combine cheeses, eggs and seasonings, fold in spinach. Spread evenly over pastry and top with remaining phyllo. Brush with melted margarine. Cover and bake 30 min.; uncover and bake until browned.

Bake: 190° (375°)
Time: 45 min
Serves: 12

Turnips and Orange

M.	Imp.	
1	1	large turnip
125 ml	1/2c	orange juice
30 ml	2T	brown sugar
1 ml	1/4t	ginger
45 ml	3T	margarine
2 ml	1/2t	salt
284 ml	1-10 oz	canned mandarin orange sections

Peel and cube the turnip. Cook in boiling salted water until done. Drain and mash. Add orange juice, brown sugar, ginger, margarine and salt. Stir well and turn into a greased casserole. Bake until heated through. Garnish with orange sections before serving.

Bake: 180° (350°)
Time: 20 min
Serves: 6

Zucchini Cheddar Casserole

M.	Imp.	
4	4	medium zucchini, sliced
250 ml	1 c	sour cream
2	2	egg yolks
25 ml	2 T	flour
2	2	egg whites, stiffly beaten
375 ml	1½ c	grated cheddar cheese
75 ml	⅓ c	toasted sesame seeds
15 ml	1 T	melted butter

Par boil zucchini 3 min. and drain. Mix together sour cream, beaten egg yolks and flour; fold in egg whites. In a shallow baking dish make layers of zucchini, egg mixture and cheese. Repeat layers and top with sesame seeds. Drizzle melted butter over all.

Bake: 180° (350°)
Time: 20 min.
Serves: 6

Some Basics

Fast Fish Stock

M.	Imp.	
1 ℓ	4c	clam nectar
1 ℓ	4c	water
½ ℓ	2c	dry white wine
2	2	slices lemon
1	1	stalk celery with leaves
1	1	onion, quartered
2	2	carrots, quartered
2	2	parsley sprigs

Combine all ingredients in a large saucepan. Simmer until reduced by 1/3. Strain. Can be frozen. Use in any fish chowder or casserole recipe calling for stock.

Old-Fashioned Soup Bags

1	1	crushed bay leaf
10 ml	2t	thyme
15 ml	3t	marjoram
45 ml	3T	dried celery leaves
3	3	cloves
2 ml	½t	peppercorns
15 ml	3t	parsley flakes
5 ml	1t	savory

Divide evenly among 3 squares of cheesecloth and tie with a string (or use large tea balls). Drop in soup for last 20 min.

Some Basics (cont'd)

Biscuit Mix

M.	Imp.	
2100 ml	9c	flour (try a mixture of whole wheat and unbleached)
60 ml	1/4c	baking powder
15 ml	1T	salt
450 g	1-lb	shortening

Stir together the flour, baking powder and salt. Cut in the shortening and use as directed: see Deep Dish Pizza, Chicken Fricassée with dumplings. Store in an airtight container. Yield: 13 cups

White Sauce Mix

225 ml	1c	flour
900 ml	4c	nonfat dry milk
225 ml	1c	margarine

Stir together the flour and milk powder. Cut in margarine as for pastry. Store in airtight container in refrigerator.

To make:	Mix	Water
thin sauce	75 ml (1/3 c) +	150 ml (2/3c)
medium sauce	120 ml (1/2 c) +	150 ml (2/3c)
thick sauce	225 ml (1 c) +	150 ml (2/3c)

Blend mix and water in a small saucepan; cook and stir over medium heat until thickened. Add salt and pepper to taste

Some Basics (cont'd)

Pie Liner I

M.	Imp.	
225 ml	1c	crushed cracker crumbs such as soda crackers, cheese flavored crackers or rusks
60 ml	1/4c	melted butter

Combine butter and crumbs; press evenly into pie plate. Yield: 1 shell

Pie Liner II

M.	Imp.	
125 ml	1/2 c	shortening
350 ml	1 1/2 c	cake and pastry flour
2 ml	1/2 t	salt
45 ml	3 T	water

Mix together 45 ml (3T) flour and the water, set aside. Stir remaining flour and salt together; cut in shortening. Drizzle the flour water mixture over flour shortening mixture, stir lightly with a fork. Gather into a ball and roll out to fit pie plate. Yield : 1 shell

Some Basics (cont'd)

Pie Liner III

450 g	1-lb	shortening
1600 ml	6 3/4 c	cake and pastry flour
20 ml	1 1/2 T	salt
175 ml	3/4 c	water

Follow the same method as Pie Liner II using 175 ml (3/4 c) flour and water for the paste. Make several pie shells for quiche, single crust pies, savory and dessert tarts

Toppers

Vary the topping for a casserole by using one of these ideas:

- buttered bread crumbs and grated cheese
- use a combination of bread crumbs and wheat germ, cornflake crumbs crushed potato chips
- to the bread crumbs add
  - bacon bits
  - chopped parsley
  - sesame seeds
  - slivered almonds / nuts
  - paprika / other seasonings
- croutons • quick croutons can be made by sautéing bread cubes in melted butter or margarine

OH NO! I'm Out of ....

Tuna ..... substitute with equal amounts of chicken, turkey, salmon, shrimp, cooked fish or diced ham

Chicken .... cooked turkey can be used in any recipe calling for cooked chicken

Celery .... substitute diced zucchini or grated carrot

Onion ..... use reconstituted dehydrated onions. Keep in mind that chopped onion freezes well.

Green pepper.. dried green pepper flakes are available or use diced celery; usually it can be omitted

Broccoli .... nothing compares to the quality of fresh vegetables but in an emergency, canned or frozen products can be used. Broccoli can be replaced with cauliflower, Brussels sprouts or a combination

Noodles.... in many instances rice can be used. Other forms of pasta can be used instead of noodles such as elbow macaroni, shell, rigatoni etc.

Rice ..... brown rice, wild rice and white rice all work equally well in casserole recipes. Try a combination for interesting texture and flavor variation. Instant rice can be used in recipes calling for cooked rice. Prepare as directed.

Cheese.... various cheeses work well in casseroles. You may want to try cheddar, swiss, parmesan, cottage cheese, jack, colby or mozzarella. Most often cheese slices can be used, too. They also make quick and tasty casserole toppers. Try freezing mixed grated cheeses ready to use for casseroles and toppings.

Oil ..... for browning meats substitute lard, butter, margarine or bacon drippings

Sour cream.. yogort can replace sour cream. Remember that the addition of either yogort or sour cream calls for heating without boiling to prevent cordling

Cream..... evaporated milk makes a satisfactory substitute. Often milk is adequate but will yield a less rich product. Dry skim milk powder reconstituted extra strength can also be used.

Parsley .... again, fresh parsley should be your first choice. If you have excess fresh parsley on hand, snip and freeze! Dried parsley flakes are available. Chervil can be used as a substitute as well

Flour..... as a thickener, cornstarch works equally well; use half the amount as for flour

Wine ...... in most recipes wine is an optional ingredient. Replace with broth in equal amounts

Calorie Counter's Checklist

Are you aware of these tips to help keep the calories down?

....drain browned meats well before adding to the recipe. In cases where the meat is placed in the casserole without browning or cooking, use lean quality meats

....when a recipe calls for seasoned flour as a coating on meats before browning, omit the flour

....use an absolute minimum of oil or bacon drippings when browning meats

....reduce margarine or butter by a half when making cream sauces

....use milk instead of cream

....you may replace sour cream with yogurt in most cases

....slightly decrease the amount of noodles or rice called for and increase the amount of vegetables

.... omit toppings when possible as they usually have high caloric content

.... cornstarch makes an excellent thickener in place of flour at half the calories. Use half the amount called for

.... many stews make superb soup-stews if left unthickened

.... use tuna packed in water rather than oil

.... rather than sautéing vegetables in butter or margarine simmer in a small amount of water

.... reduce the amount of salt called for

.... slightly reduce the amount of cheese called for

.... omit the pie liner for quiches

.... replace mayonnaise with half the amount of milk plus a little lemon juice

Books in the Just Series